TAMBA HALI

Get in the game with your favorite athletes:

BECKY SAUERBRUNN

REAL SPORTS CONTENT NETWORK PRESENTS

TAMBA HALI

David Seigerman

ALADDIN

NEW YORK LONDON TORONTO SYDNEY NEW DELHI

ALADDIN

An imprint of Simon & Schuster Children's Publishing Division

1230 Avenue of the Americas, New York, New York 10020

First Aladdin hardcover edition November 2017

Text copyright © 2017 by Real Content Media Group

Jacket photograph copyright © 2017 by Peter G. Aiken/Getty Images

Also available in an Aladdin paperback edition.

For information about special discounts for bulk purchases, please contact
Simon & Schuster Special Sales at 1-866-506-1949 or business@simonandschuster.com.

The Simon & Schuster Speakers Bureau can bring authors to your live event. For more
information or to book an event contact the Simon & Schuster Speakers Bureau at
1-866-248-3049 or visit our website at www.simonspeakers.com.

Book designed by Greg Stadnyk

The text of this book was set in Caecilia.

Manufactured in the United States of America 1017 FFG

2 4 6 8 10 9 7 5 3 1

Library of Congress Cataloging-in-Publication Data

Names: Seigerman, David, author. Title: Tamba Hali / By David Seigerman.

Description: New York : Aladdin, 2017. | Series: Real Sports Content Network Presents |
Includes bibliographical references and index. | Audience: Age 8-12. | Description based
on print version record and CIP data provided by publisher; resource not viewed.

Identifiers: LCCN 2017002976 (print) | LCCN 2017012276 (eBook) |
ISBN 9781481482219 (eBook) | ISBN 9781481482202 (hc) | ISBN 9781481482196 (pbk)

Subjects: LCSH: Hali, Tamba, 1983—Juvenile literature. | Football players—United States—
Biography—Juvenile literature. | Liberian Americans—Biography—Juvenile literature. |
Liberia—Biography—Juvenile literature. | BISAC: JUVENILE NONFICTION / Biography &
Autobiography / Sports & Recreation. | JUVENILE NONFICTION / Sports & Recreation /
Football. | JUVENILE NONFICTION / People & Places / United States / African American.

Classification: LCC GV939.H275 (eBook) | LCC GV939.H275 S45 2017 (print) |
DDC 796.332092 [B]—dc23

LC record available at https://lccn.loc.gov/2017002976

This book is dedicated to children around the world, all of whom, regardless of circumstance, deserve the chance to dream of what they one day may become.

CONTENTS

TAMBA HALI:
THE BASICS

BIRTHDAY: November 3, 1983

BIRTHPLACE: Gbarnga, Liberia, Africa

ADOPTED HOMETOWN: Teaneck, New Jersey

PRIMARY POSITION: Tamba spent his first three professional seasons playing defensive end in Kansas City's 4–3 system (which uses four defensive linemen, three linebackers). When the Chiefs moved to a 3–4 defense (three linemen, four linebackers), Tamba moved to outside linebacker, where he has been ever since. Regardless of his position, his primary responsibility hasn't changed: Tamba Hali's job, first and foremost, is to rush the quarterback.

CURRENT TEAM: Kansas City Chiefs

COLLEGE: Penn State University (2002–2006)

SHORT LIST OF FOOTBALL ACHIEVEMENTS: *High School*: recorded 20 sacks, 109 solo tackles, and 47 tackles for loss in his last two seasons at Teaneck (N. J.) High School; named High School All-American by *SuperPrep*, which also ranked him as the third-best defensive lineman prospect in the nation and the top college prospect at any position in the state of New Jersey. *College*: Consensus first-team All-American and Big Ten Defensive Lineman of the Year as a senior in 2005, when he registered 11 sacks, 17 tackles for loss, and 65 total tackles; finalist for the Nagurski Trophy (awarded to the nation's top defender) and Ted Hendricks Award (top defensive lineman) in 2005; finished his career top ten in Penn State history in both sacks and tackles for loss; named Defensive MVP at the 2006 Senior Bowl. *Professional:* First-round draft pick (twentieth) overall in 2006; led the American Football Conference [AFC] in sacks in 2010 (14.5); finished the 2016 season ranked second in the Chiefs record books in career quarterback sacks (86.0) and second in forced fumbles (33); selected to the Pro Bowl five straight seasons (2011–2015).

NICKNAME: The Tamba Hawk, a Chiefs-themed nickname (based on the "tomahawk") given to him by his former teammate Jared Allen. It describes the way Tamba celebrates a sack—by spreading his arms to their full wingspan, like a hawk soaring above its prey. Also, whenever an opposing team is in an obvious passing situation, it's known around

Arrowhead Stadium as Tamba Time—meaning time for Hali to rack up another sack.

WORDS TO LIVE BY: Few players endured the highs and lows of college football that Tamba did. During his sophomore and junior seasons at Penn State, Tamba and his Nittany Lions teammates won seven games. *Combined.* Those 2002–2003 seasons resulted in the worst records of Joe Paterno's forty-six seasons as Penn State head coach.

Then, in Tamba's senior season, the Lions went 11–1 and won the Orange Bowl. What did Tamba learn from that roller-coaster ride of a college career? "I watched how Joe went about everything, and that taught me a lot. When you are doing good, there's a feeling that you're on top of everything. That's not true; it's just a facade. And when you're losing, you think you're the worst. You're not. The way you handle criticism and praise is you keep them in the same box. And how you handle both situations says more about your character than anything you will do as a player."

IF IT WEREN'T FOR SPORTS . . . You might still have heard of Tamba Hali, but not on sports radio. Maybe you'd be hearing from him on Hot 97, the New York–based radio station ("Where Hip-Hop Lives"). It's the station Tamba listened to growing up in Teaneck, when he dreamed not of becoming a New York Giant, but a New York giant like his favorite rappers, Biggie Smalls, LL Cool J, and Jay Z. Back in Africa, Tamba first learned to play the drums—specifically, the *djembe*, which is a West African drum similar to a bongo. In college, Tamba started to dabble in writing poetry, which, over time, developed into writing lyrics. In fact, in early 2016, he recorded and released a few rap songs on his own SoundCloud page. One of those original songs was "Look What I Started," in which he references both his difficult early life in Liberia and his success in the National Football League [NFL]. Don't be surprised if you hear more from Tamba the musician once his playing days are done.

CHAPTER 1

WELCOME TO THE RED SEA

In the bright sunshine of a beautiful autumn Sunday, the red helmets of the Kansas City Chiefs glistened like candy apples. It was eighty-two degrees at midday, almost as if summer had packed its bags but decided not to leave when fall officially arrived a week and a day earlier. It was a perfect day for football.

As usual, the stands at Arrowhead Stadium were packed. From the blimp shot high above the stadium, the scene, with fans dressed in home team red and white, looked like a giant candy dish overflowing with peppermints. It was a typical Chiefs crowd: large, lively, and loud.

Kansas City loud is different from the kind of loud you hear in most football stadiums. Once, in 1990, Denver's Hall of Fame quarterback John Elway found himself pinned back to his own goal line, and the Chiefs fans were loving it, cheering so loudly that Elway couldn't hear himself shouting instructions at the line of scrimmage. Twice he was forced to turn to the officials for help, unable to get the ball snapped to start the play. The referee actually had to address the crowd, like a parent scolding a teenager to *turn that music down or else!* He warned that another noise-related interruption would result in a delay of game penalty against the Chiefs.

That was no one-time incident. Kansas City is known for its unique brands of jazz and barbecue, and sometimes it is referred to as the City of Fountains; in football circles, though, it's known more for its shoutin'. In 2014, the Chiefs invited a representative from Guinness World Records to a Monday Night Football game against New England. The fans were planning to reset a record that had long belonged to them before being stolen by the Seattle Seahawks—the Loudest Crowd Roar at a Sports Stadium. Sure enough, during a play stoppage, the Chiefs faithful reclaimed their title, cheering at an ear-splitting 142.2 decibels (a scientific measure of volume). By comparison, if you were fifty feet away from a military jet taking off from the deck of an aircraft carrier, that would only register at about 130 decibels—as loud as a two-hundred-person marching band. Chiefs fans were louder than that. Any louder and your eyesight could go blurry, because your eyeballs would vibrate from the sound waves. Seriously.

Kansas City fans are loud and proud. But when they flocked to Arrowhead on October 1, 2006, they hadn't had much to cheer about recently.

Sure, sports fans on the other side of the state

were pretty happy. The St. Louis Cardinals used a three-run rally the day before to beat the Milwaukee Brewers. One more win and the Cards would clinch the National League Central Division and qualify for the playoffs (which, by the way, they did . . . on their way to winning the World Series that year).

Back in Kansas City, though, the only things looking rosy were the Chiefs jerseys. Their own baseball team, the Royals, was lousy, stumbling to another last place finish and finishing off the worst three-year stretch in their history. Since the start of September, football season had no competition in the sports pages or the hearts of Kansas City fans.

Things were supposed to be better for the Chiefs, but so far they were not. Kansas City entered the 2006 season with a new head coach. Dick Vermeil had retired back on New Year's Day after failing to reach the playoffs the year before, despite a 10–6 record. He had been replaced by Herman Edwards, the former New York Jets coach, who had been a Chiefs assistant coach ten years earlier. Edwards brought his trademark positive energy and motivational rhetoric to his new job, but even his optimism must have been tested in those early days.

The Chiefs lost their first two games of the 2006 season. Even worse, they had lost their starting quarterback—Trent Green, a Pro Bowl quarterback. He had thrown for more than four thousand yards in three straight seasons—a pretty rare accomplishment—and was a key to the Chiefs' hopes for a successful season. But in the second half of the first game, Green was knocked out. Literally. He was scrambling with the ball and was starting to slide to avoid a tackle when his head collided first with the shoulder of a defender and then with the ground. Green was knocked unconscious, and the game was stopped for fifteen minutes while doctors and trainers attended to him. Green had suffered what was later called a "very, very severe concussion" (medical note: It's never good when someone uses the word "very" in describing an injury), and he would be sidelined until mid-November.

As they prepared to play the San Francisco 49ers on October 1—on their home turf, in front of their loud crowd—the Chiefs were 0–2. Perhaps the only reason they weren't 0–3 was that they had a bye in Week Three, meaning they had a week off, which they desperately needed to try to get their new starting quarterback, Damon Huard, ready to play. Before replacing Green in Week One, Huard hadn't completed an NFL pass in six years.

There were a few positive signs, though, if you knew where to look. Kansas City's star running back, Larry Johnson, had rushed for 126 yards in Week Two against the Broncos. The team's defense, steadily improving since being second worst in the league two years earlier, was playing well. They hadn't allowed a touchdown in six quarters.

And fans were getting their first taste of the team's first-round draft pick, a defensive end from Penn State named Tamba Hali.

Much of the attention during the buildup to the 2006 NFL Draft was focused on the quarterbacks. Fans across the league were wondering where Matt Leinart, a former Heisman Trophy winner from USC, and Vince Young, the Heisman runner-up and the quarterback who led Texas to the national championship, would wind up. On draft night, however, the drama centered on the surprise top two picks.

Houston stunned many draft experts by selecting Maryland defensive end Mario Williams instead of USC do-it-all running back Reggie Bush, the Heisman Trophy winner. Second-guessing began as soon as the first pick was made, and it hadn't subsided much by the time the Chiefs were on the clock with pick number twenty.

Commissioner Paul Tagliabue stepped to the podium and announced the Chiefs' pick, and Hali's unique journey to professional football had taken its next step.

Kansas City fans might not have known much about Tamba's background. Maybe they'd heard that he was born in the West African country of Liberia and that he hadn't played a snap of football before high school. More likely, they probably knew that he was a consensus first-team All-American, which means every publication, association, and media outlet named him to their All-America lists after the 2005 season. Chances are they looked up his stats— 65 tackles, a forced fumble, and 11 sacks (most among any defender in the Big Ten Conference)— and figured the Chiefs had drafted another pass rusher to bookend the one they already had. Jared Allen was a third-year defensive end who had 20 sacks in his first two NFL seasons. At least the fans knew more about Hali than they had about Allen when Kansas City drafted him out of Idaho State in the fourth round two years earlier.

Some draft analysts felt the pick was a bit of a reach, speculating that Hali might not be one of the twenty best players available in the draft class. Others felt it was a solid pick, especially if Hali continued to develop the way he did at Penn State. After all, he had only played two seasons at defensive end.

The rookie showed his new coaches enough during training camp to earn a starting job. Indeed, he was the Chiefs' starting left defensive end those first two games of the 2006 season. And while he didn't have a sack, he made 11 tackles. If Hali hadn't yet given the Chiefs fans something to crow about, he certainly hadn't given them anything to complain about either.

And so Kansas City's faithful, full-throated fans filed into Arrowhead that first day of October in a happy, hopeful mood. And why not? The 49ers team they would see that day had lost two of its first three games. This wasn't exactly the

Joe Montana–Jerry Rice Niners of San Francisco's glory days. Maybe there were a few more empty seats than normal, but that wasn't because anyone was down on the Chiefs—there was a NASCAR race, the Banquet 400, being run at the same time at the Kansas Speedway, located in the "other half" of Kansas City, a few miles across the border into Kansas. But those who were on hand were ready for their beloved Chiefs to turn their season around.

Coach Edwards's team wasted little time in giving the home crowd reason to cheer. They took the ball first, went seventy-three yards in ten plays, scored a touchdown, and took a 7–0 lead. A much-needed good start.

Hali and Allen and the Chiefs defense took the field for the first time of the afternoon. San Francisco had a powerful running back of its own, Frank Gore, and he hammered straight ahead for five yards on the first play against the Kansas City defense. On second down and five yards to go for a first down, San Francisco quarterback Alex Smith dropped back to pass. And Tamba Hali officially introduced himself to Arrowhead Stadium.

When the ball was snapped, Hali charged at the man assigned to block him: 49ers right tackle, Kwame Harris. At six feet, seven inches tall, he was four inches taller than Hali; Harris also outweighed Hali by about forty-five pounds. Unconcerned, Hali exploded into his blocker, forcing the bigger man back onto his heels. He then accelerated to his left and blew past Harris, once honored as the top offensive lineman in the PAC-10 Conference, and made a beeline toward the quarterback.

At the thirty-two-yard line, Hali clobbered Alex Smith's throwing arm with his left hand. The ball dropped from Smith's hands and started to bounce away. The quarterback was able to recover the loose ball at the thirty-five-yard line, but he was down and the play was dead. And Tamba Hali had just recorded the first sack and the first forced fumble of his NFL career all on the same play.

Arrowhead Stadium erupted. A red sea of fans began hollering its appreciation for their first-round rookie, and it wouldn't be the last time either. Hali would share another sack later in the game with linebacker Derrick Johnson (the team's first-round pick the year before), and the Chiefs would go on to demolish the 49ers, 41–0. They would win seven of their next nine games, finish the regular season with a record of 9–7, and return to the playoffs.

Over the next decade, Tamba Hali would collect more quarterback sacks than any player in team history except the legendary Derrick Thomas. Not as many as Jared Allen would have before he retired in 2015 (long after he had left the Chiefs) or as many as Mario Williams, that controversial first pick in 2006. But Hali would move into the top fifty of the NFL's all-time list of quarterback sacks.

On that day 77,609 people were on hand to witness that first sack of Tamba Hali's career. One of them, seated in the end zone, overwhelmed by the noise and the colors in the stands and the violence on the field, was Rachel Keita.

She had never been to a football game before, hadn't watched much more than the occasional highlight on television. She didn't know the rules of the game, though she could follow the crowd's reaction to tell when something good had happened. Like Hali's sack of Alex Smith.

Rachel had been watching the San Francisco quarterback. That's what she had been instructed to do: "Keep your eyes on the quarterback. My job is to get him."

That's what Tamba Hali had told her a few days earlier, after she arrived in America from West Africa to see her son for the first time in twelve years. The last time they were together, he was a ten-year-old boy, and their family was trying to escape the bloody civil war tearing Liberia apart.

Now, a dozen years later, her Tamba—in the

tradition of the Kissi tribe, that was the name given to a woman's second son—was a grown man, six feet three, 265 pounds, wearing a candy-apple-red helmet and a jersey to match, with his last name on the back. People in the stands were wearing the same jersey, some with his number 91 on it. And right now, right in front of Rachel, who was awe-struck and unsure what to make of this spectacle, they were standing on their feet and cheering her son's name.

CHAPTER 2

THE STORM

On Christmas Day 1989, everything changed.

Tamba Hali was a little more than six years old that day, living with his mother and stepfather and siblings in a humble home in the Liberian city of Gbarnga. It may not have been a place of prosperity, but it was peaceful. Until the storm came.

In fact, that's exactly what Tamba and his family first thought they were hearing. It sounded like the faint rumblings of a faraway thunderstorm, and they listened to see if it might be headed their way.

It was. Slowly. But it was no thunderstorm. It was the coming of war.

Before you can appreciate what thirteen years of civil war would do to Tamba Hali's world, you first have to understand a little bit about the place he called home.

Liberia is a country in the southwesternmost corner of West Africa, a region once regarded as the Pepper Coast, named for the *melegueta* pepper that grew exclusively there. Tucked between Sierra Leone, Guinea, and Ivory Coast, it ends right where the African coastline takes a hard turn toward the east, a few latitudinal clicks above the equator, where the North Atlantic and the South Atlantic meet and go their separate ways.

Liberia covers about forty-three thousand square miles within its jagged borders, roughly the size of the state of Virginia. With a population of approximately 4.5 million, it's comparable to Kentucky or Louisiana.

There's a boat (much like the one that delivered them from bondage to freedom), a shovel and plow (which depict the hard work of building a new life), a rising sun (a new day), a white dove (the symbol of peace dating back to the days of Noah and his ark), and a palm tree. It is thought that the tree symbolizes prosperity; in time, the tree came to mean something profoundly different for the people of Liberia.

From the beginning, English has been the official language of Liberia. This is somewhat surprising, since the colonists from America and the Caribbean represented only about 5 percent of the population. Most people were indigenous—meaning that they lived already in the land, like the Native Americans who were already in North America when the Europeans arrived—and belonged to any one of sixteen different ethnic groups, each with its own traditions, histories, religious beliefs, and in many cases, languages. But English prevailed, thanks entirely to the relationship between Liberia and its original friend to the west, America.

Even Liberia's capital—the coastal city of Monrovia—has American roots. It is named for James Monroe, the fifth president of the United States, who was in office when the first freed African-American slaves returned to Africa. The resettlement began in the 1820s; by the time the American Civil War ended forty-five years later, more than thirteen thousand former slaves from the West had been relocated to Liberia.

Fast forward a century or so. By 1980, the Republic of Liberia had grown, slowly, into a participating member of the international community. It had supported the Allies during World War II and was one of a few African countries to join the United Nations when it was founded in 1945.

But in the spring of 1980, the government of Liberia was overthrown. Until that time, the president of Liberia had always been an Americo

Liberian—someone descended from the African-American slaves who colonized Liberia from the start. For the first time, the new leader came from one of those many ethnic groups that made up the population.

The 1980s became a turbulent time, with several more attempted coups d'état—which means a violent overthrow of a government. During those years, the Liberian president, Samuel Doe, retaliated against the tribes and territories where those plotters were from. Animosity between these ethnic groups escalated. Violence flared, the economy faltered. Liberia was a cauldron of unrest and mistrust and discontent—a deadly brew—and for a decade it bubbled steadily toward the point of boiling over.

The flash point came on Christmas 1989.

While Tamba Hali and his family prepared to celebrate the birth of Jesus (a big day throughout the country, as Liberia is primarily a Christian

nation), a revolution-minded ex-government official named Charles Taylor was leading a small army
of rebels from Ivory Coast into Liberia. Not much
more than a hundred men marched into Nimba
County on December 25, 1989, and soon the haunt-
ing sounds of explosions could be heard next door
in Bong County, where the Hali children played on
Christmas Day.

War didn't come to Gbarnga right away. The
rumors arrived well before the soldiers, though they
were nearly as terrifying. Taylor's rebels, known as
the National Patriotic Front of Liberia (NPFL) were
brutalizing the villages on their way to Monrovia,
where they intended to overthrow President Doe.
In 1980, it was Doe who rose to power after his men
assassinated the sitting president and many of his
government's top leaders. Now, he was the target
of this new coup. Battle lines between the different ethnic groups were hardening, like scratches
in drying concrete that would become permanent

and impossible to erase. The First Liberian Civil War had begun.

Through the winter of 1990, the residents of Gbarnga remained on alert, listening for the sounds of war to creep closer. They were not yet in harm's way, but they knew it was a matter of time.

For the Hali family and their neighbors and friends, the life they had known was over. Everything had changed, like a dark cloud had come out of nowhere to swallow up a glowing sun and permanently darken the blue sky. If they had woken up one morning to find that fish could walk and birds swim, it would not have been more stunning or sudden. They had entered a new reality, where fear now hung over everyone everywhere every day.

"All young people were forced to grow up in a matter of moments," said Saah Hali, who is a year older than his brother, Tamba.

Soon enough, many of their neighbors began packing up their clothes and few belongings, boarding up their homes, and leaving town. Military vehicles appeared from time to time, and villagers would not know whether it was the Liberian armed forces or the rebels. They soon would come to learn that it really didn't matter. When the war came, they were in danger from all sides.

CHAPTER 3

HIDING IN THE BUSH

There are things that happen in a war that are unimaginable to anyone who hasn't witnessed one. In some ways, the Liberian civil war was different—maybe even worse than traditional military conflicts. Reports of the atrocities committed by and against civilians during that war—some acts done willingly, others coerced at gunpoint—are horrifying. Even scarier is the fact that some were committed not by adults, but by the thousands of children who were forced to fight as rebel soldiers.

This book isn't the place to recount those

inhuman acts. It's enough for you to realize that the kinds of things that would give you nightmares just to read about, Tamba Hali lived through between the ages of six and nine years old. The ghost stories of his childhood were not spooky tales saved for campfires. There were no imaginary bogeymen under his bed or skulking in his closet. His monsters were real. And they were everywhere.

In early 1990, the war had reached all the way to Gbarnga. Tamba's family knew it was finally time to leave. They boarded up their home and, carrying what they could manage, Tamba and his extended family—his mother and stepfather, his siblings (half and full), cousins and uncles and aunts—climbed into the back of a transport truck with twenty other people from their town and fled to a safer village deeper in the countryside.

For people fleeing for their lives, there was safety in numbers. There was also danger.

If they were to encounter rebel soldiers along

the journey, anyone in the group might be questioned about their loyalties or their tribal background. At the time, the rebels were hunting primarily for Krahn people. President Doe was of Krahn descent, and he tended to show favoritism toward the Krahn people, often at the expense of other ethnic groups. That's what lit the fuse for Taylor's coup. Gun-wielding rebels might ask one person out of a truckload of twenty whether they were Krahn; the wrong answer could get everyone killed. Even if the person told the truth about his or her background, the armed inquisitor might choose not to believe that person. Life and death depended on a soldier's mood.

That scenario was a very real risk for Tamba and his family. His stepfather was from the Mandingo tribe, which was another population targeted by the rebels. That reality put everyone he traveled with in jeopardy.

"They might think everyone with him was

Mandingo, too," said Saah. "That would be the end of the story."

Fortunately for Tamba and his family, no one learned his stepfather's secret, and they were able to find refuge in another town. Tamba has vague memories of that time, settling into a mud hut when his family first escaped Gbarnga. It was a small dwelling with two or three rooms. Ten people, maybe a dozen, would live there together, with all the children—usually seven or eight, often more—sleeping on the floor of one of the rooms. Their sleeping bodies were crammed together like jigsaw-puzzle pieces, covering the floor like a breathing carpet. A bed was a luxury, like running water or toilets or electricity, that Tamba didn't even dare to dream about.

After six months or so, relatively good news reached Tamba and his family at their temporary home. The war had moved on from Gbarnga; it was safe to return.

Some homes in the area had been destroyed when the soldiers passed through. Virtually all had been looted. Any possessions left behind had been taken or broken. Still, Tamba had a house to come home to, and his family could attempt to return to their normal lives. Children can be amazingly resilient, even under the most difficult of circumstances, and soon enough Tamba was back to fishing and swimming and kicking around a soccer ball with his friends—back to being a kid.

That is how the next two years went for Tamba Hali and his family. They would live safely on the periphery of the war, until they weren't safe and they had to go back into hiding. When it was deemed safe to return home, they would . . . until the next wave of violence crashed down on them and sent them running again. Maybe they would be in hiding for days, maybe for months. Whenever they left home, they had no idea when they might be back.

Sometimes the threat was the rebels, with their AK-47 rifles and their viciousness. Sometimes it was the president's men, whose planes began to pass over Gbarnga with increasing regularity. In fact, the first time Tamba experienced actual gunfire, it came from the sky. He was in the road when an F-16 swooped down and opened fire on the villagers. They figured anyone out in the open could have been a rebel soldier. Even a six-year-old boy like Tamba. The Liberian military took no chances, so they shot at whoever was outside and beneath their flight path.

This became an all too common occurrence. The planes might come at three o'clock in the morning or at nine o'clock at night, interrupting the night with noise from their engines or their weapons. Either way, no one in the village would be able to sleep.

One day, the F-16s returned for a daytime bombing run. Everyone outdoors at the time scattered and scrambled for safety. Tamba knew his mother had been cooking rice for the family meal. Instead of running for cover, he ran to save the food. He knew they might need it if they went into hiding, and his sharpened survival instincts drove him to protect the precious food. Tamba Hali was figuring out how to live through a war—lessons no child should have to learn.

That's really what every day boiled down to for Tamba and his family, and for most of Liberia's two million residents: find something to eat and survive the day. "For me, that was what the world was about, the two main reasons for living," Tamba said.

That was easy enough to manage during those intermittent periods when the world was safe and stable enough for families to be living in their homes. Hiding in the bush, however, provided an entirely different set of challenges.

Let's be clear: Hiding in the bush is exactly what it sounds like. People forced to evacuate their homes and villages would take to the forests for cover. Remember the palm tree from the Liberian coat of arms? It no longer stood for prosperity; now, a palm tree meant protection.

They would avoid walking on the roads, where they might be mistaken for rebels and targeted by F-16 raids. Or they might encounter actual rebels who might kill or kidnap them. Or they could confront "official" government checkpoints where they often were forced to bribe the guards with money or food or clothes in order to pass. Once, Tamba was traveling in another crowded truck through a new security checkpoint. The guards let them through, but then someone opened fire on the truck. Tamba jumped up, waving his arms and screaming, "Don't shoot!" His older half brother, also named Tamba, yanked him down and back into the safety of the truck.

"When you're that age," Tamba said, "you don't know what's happening or why it's all happening to you."

So they would find hiding places in the forests—the one resource that Liberia had plenty to offer. At the start of the civil war, roughly 45 percent of Liberia was forest; after thirteen years of fighting, the country had lost approximately 13 percent of its forest and close to 70 percent of its coastal mangrove swamps. Thanks to "conflict timber"—trees that were cut down and sold by Taylor's forces to help finance the rebel militias—Liberia's rain forests were an underreported casualty of the violence. The war killed not only Liberia's people but its land as well.

Of the many kinds of trees common to the Liberian bush, banana trees offered some of the best hiding spots. They could grow as tall as twenty-five feet. Their leaves could reach nine feet long and two feet wide; they grew next to one another, almost like the blades of a ceiling fan, which provided a natural umbrella of protection from above.

Banana trees often grew in dense swampy areas, which also became a common place for people to hide. Of course, they were not without their special challenges. Mosquitoes thrive in swampy conditions, and in West Africa, mosquitoes are notorious for carrying deadly diseases, such as malaria and dengue fever. Hiding in the swamps, people could be a little safer from bullets but not from bugs.

Swamps also were home to leeches, which were decidedly the lesser of two evils. "Not much of a choice," Saah said. "You can risk getting infested with leeches and have to seek some sort of medical help, or you get shot at."

Medical help, of course, was not exactly easy to come by. Clinics and hospitals throughout the country were destroyed over the course of the war, making it increasingly difficult to treat the sick, the wounded, and the dying. Tamba witnessed people being shot in the legs having to be tended to in the bush by what he called "old remedies," which often weren't enough to fight off infection.

Clean drinking water wasn't readily available,

nor were sanitary conditions for bathing and other bathroom-related needs.

And what about food?

"Everywhere we went, we lived off the land," Tamba said.

There were bananas and mangoes. There were rice and potatoes. There was sugarcane. And there was cassava, a plant whose root could be eaten as well as the leaves. These already were staples of the Liberian diet, though ample amounts could be difficult to find while hiding. Nobody ate until they were full or even satisfied. They ate for survival.

"You would eat as much as you could to maintain yourself," Saah said. "After that, if you had anything, you gave it to other people."

Malnutrition can become a big problem for people living in the bush for weeks at a time, especially for babies and young children and the elderly. Meat, and the protein it provided, was scarce. Sometimes, they would be able to fish or send a party out to hunt for deer or other animals that could be caught in the wild. That could mean a supper menu featuring rodents or fruit bats or snakes.

"Guys would go out hunting and come back with a huge snake," Tamba said. "That was a meal."

Of course, some of the food came with health risks. Poorly cooked meats could sicken someone, as would undercooked palm roots (an occasional substitute for cassava). Simply coming into contact with infected animals could bring disease, potentially putting the cook at greater risk than the people eating the food. Fruit bats were considered to be a primary carrier of the Ebola virus that in 2014 killed more than eleven thousand people across West Africa. Liberia and its neighbors, Sierra Leone and Guinea, were the epicenter of the epidemic. That's who the refugees shared the bush with.

Tamba and his family and neighbors lived like this for days, weeks, even months at a time. Hiding in the bush until the fighting left town, returning home until the threat returned, then back to the bush.

Meanwhile, the war was growing more chaotic. Back in September 1990, President Doe had been captured, tortured, and killed, but that didn't end the fighting. A different rebel group had splintered away from the Charles Taylor–led NPFL, calling itself the Independent National Patriotic Front of Liberia (INPFL). The INPFL was responsible for Doe's death. But now these two growing armies were fighting for control of Monrovia and power over all of Liberia.

An intervention force, formed by sixteen different neighboring countries, also had entered the fray. It was called the Economic Community of West African States Monitoring Group (ECOMOG). Eventually, Doe's supporters reconstituted as the United Liberation Movement of Liberia for Democracy (ULIMO) and rejoined the fight, though it, too, would split into two groups—one primarily Krahn, the other mostly Mandingo.

Liberia had become one giant alphabet soup of death and devastation. Hiding in the bush no longer seemed like a safe enough option. By the fall of 1992, Tamba Hali's family decided that their homeland was lost. The time had come to leave Liberia.

CHAPTER *4*

THE CROSSING

One hundred and sixty-three years after the first Liberians arrived from America, Henry Hali made the return trip.

Tamba Hali's father was an educated man. He had studied math and chemistry at Cuttington University, located in the Suakoko District of Bong County, just to the northwest of Gbarnga on the way toward Monrovia. It was one of the oldest private four-year colleges on the African continent. Many of the leaders of Liberia's government in the 1980s were educated at Cuttington.

Henry was a learner and a teacher, and he didn't like the direction he saw his country headed in. So, in 1985, he left for the original Land of the Free—the United States—where he hoped to set up residency and be able to bring his family someday, ideally before conditions in Liberia deteriorated any further. He left behind his four children, two of whom he fathered with Rachel Keita, and two from previous relationships. Tamba Hali and his siblings—full sister Kumba, and half brothers Tamba (who was twelve years older) and Saah (one year older)—were cared for by his mother, Rachel, and their stepfather, a pastor.

Big Tamba, as the oldest brother was called, assumed a father-figure role for the younger children, especially for Little Tamba (odd, isn't it, to think that an NFL linebacker would be considered "Little Tamba" in his own family?). He was eighteen years old when the war broke out; two years later, it was a twenty-year-old Big Tamba who helped his brothers leave Liberia.

Rachel, Kumba, and Tamba's stepfather left first, headed for Ivory Coast. The three boys remained behind, planning to follow them soon and reconnect across the border around the city of Danané.

It wasn't long before it was the boys' turn to go. One day, Big Tamba was down the hill from his family's home in Gbarnga where he was greeted with some startling news. "Someone told me, 'Tamba says he wants to go fight,'" Big Tamba said.

This couldn't have come as a total surprise. Child soldiers at checkpoints were always trying to recruit kids their own age. They had guns and confidence and always seemed to be the ones in control of these tense standoffs—why wouldn't that appeal to an eight- or nine-year-old boy on the run?

Apparently, Tamba had seen someone his age in the village with an AK-47 who had decided to join the war. Now, for the first time, Tamba was expressing an interest in joining too.

Big Tamba knew he'd reached a critical crossroads. He couldn't deprive his brother of the chance to fight, if that was indeed his choice. But he couldn't allow his brother to do it, either.

"I told him, 'You gotta kill me first,'" Big Tamba said.

That gave Tamba enough pause for Big Tamba to act. One morning soon thereafter, shortly after 5 a.m., the three Hali boys climbed into a crowded car for the daylong drive to the border.

Leaving Liberia was the last choice most families wanted to make, but it was the decision so many of them ultimately arrived at. It is estimated that over the course of thirteen years of war— which encompassed the First and Second Liberian Civil Wars and the brief pocket of relative peace that separated them—virtually all of the country's two to three million inhabitants were displaced at some point. More than two hundred thousand Liberians died. Several hundred thousand more would leave the country, flooding into Sierra Leone, Guinea, and Ivory Coast. In 1996 alone, more than 780,000 refugees had fled beyond Liberia's borders—roughly one out of every three people in the country was gone.

Escaping the country was no easier than hiding in the bush. Many families began their flight without any warning or time to prepare. Bullets would start to fly and people fled. Family members would become separated in the chaos; often they would not be able to find one another again or know which relatives had even survived the attack.

The roads to the border, of course, remained treacherous. Along the way, refugees would file through checkpoint after checkpoint, some separated by no more than a mile or so. It became like driving through a suburban development, where there are stop signs at every intersection. It was slow going, and every checkpoint offered a new danger.

So much of the land had been captured by rebels, retaken by the government forces, then reclaimed by rebels or some other warlords. Control of any area likely changed hands so many times, people didn't know who would be waiting for them at a given checkpoint. Or what would be required of them as payment. Villages that were safe one day were hot spots the next. Passing through them was like running a race where the finish line kept changing on you.

Once people reached the border, the crossing became no easier. Official checkpoints were manned by people with one hand holding a gun and the other hand extended, awaiting some sort of bribe or "toll." Many people chose to cross the border where it might be unguarded, which often meant crossing a river either by swimming, in some makeshift canoe, or by clinging to a floating tree or fallen branch. Not an insubstantial number of Liberians survived the long journey to the border, only to drown meters from their destination. Tamba, Big Tamba, and Saah would not have to risk a river crossing. They would take their chances at a guarded checkpoint.

They spent seven hours that day jammed into a taxi already stuffed with passengers. Every seat was full, as was every lap. When they arrived at the border, Big Tamba instructed the younger boys to keep walking while he talked to the guards. Tamba didn't want to leave his brother's side. He and Saah were afraid something would happen and they would get across only to be stranded in a foreign place without their big brother, their protector.

The two younger brothers watched as Big Tamba began his negotiation with the soldiers at the border with a promise: *If you let me take my brothers across and drop them off, I will come back and bring you food. Anything you want.*

The guards—who probably were as hungry as everyone else in the starving country—were intrigued but unconvinced. Ultimately, it was an American president who did the trick: Ulysses S. Grant, whose face is on the fifty-dollar bill.

There is a superstition among gamblers and even some casinos in the United States that a fifty-dollar bill is unlucky. But for the Hali brothers at the border between Liberia and Ivory Coast, it was the Golden Ticket.

They were allowed to cross. Before they did, Tamba saw a dead body off to the side—one last glimpse into the killing fields their country had become. It wasn't the first he'd seen, but this one at this place provided one sharp, final reminder of the world and the war they were leaving behind.

"When we got to the border," Big Tamba said, "it was up to the grace of God. He gave me the wisdom to say what I needed to say to get us to the other side."

The boys walked a short distance until they found cars waiting to take refugees from the border to the city. Shortly after they arrived, they were reunited with the rest of their family—a joyous experience not all refugee families had the good fortune to share.

Soon after, Big Tamba found himself on a long line at a local pay phone. Everyone who had made it out of Liberia, it seemed, had someone to call somewhere else in the world. And every one of them, it seemed, was ahead of him in line.

Eventually, he got to the front and placed a call to a phone number on the other side of an ocean. Until he answered the ringing phone a world away, Henry Hali had not spoken with his children since the war began and Gbarnga was essentially cut off from communicating with the rest of the world.

That conversation began for Henry the long process of bringing his children to America. First, he flew to Ivory Coast to see his children, but his request to take them home with him was rejected by the officials charged with deciding who was allowed to live in the United States and who was not.

It took about two years of paperwork and waiting, and no small financial investment. Red tape doesn't come cheap. Finally, the rubber stamps came through and Tamba and his siblings were given the green light to join their father in the United States.

Rachel was not. Since she was not married to Henry, she was not considered his immediate family, so she didn't qualify for the appropriate visa. She would remain behind indefinitely.

After she said good-bye to them at the airport, she would not speak to her children much for the next twelve years. And she wouldn't see her son Tamba again until he was a grown man with a job in the National Football League, a contract worth several million dollars (that's a lot of Grants), and American citizenship.

On September 15, 1994, Tamba Hali, Big Tamba, Saah, and Kumba found themselves on an airplane, the Pepper Coast shrinking into the distance. They were bound first for a stopover in Portugal and then on to a new life in a new world. Their new home offered such a fresh start, it even had "new" in its name: New Jersey.

CHAPTER 5

TACKLING A NEW LIFE

Flying into Newark airport can be disconcerting for anyone, even a seasoned traveler. It is, after all, the busiest of the three international airports in the New York metropolitan area, which is the second busiest area in the world for airline traffic. In 1994, twenty-eight million passengers flew into, out of, or had a layover in Newark. Few could have been more bug-eyed and awestruck than Tamba Hali and his siblings when their wheels touched down in the least gardeny part of the Garden State.

All the planes, the people, the pace ... Just walking through the terminal and seeing all the restaurant choices would have been enough to wobble their knees. It's no wonder Tamba says he felt like he'd gone from zero to one hundred miles an hour in an instant. It may have taken a long time to get them to their destination, but suddenly, they were in America, fifteen miles from the Statue of Liberty, whose engraved invitation must have felt as if it were extended to them personally. The homeless and tempest tossed had landed in New Jersey, a state whose motto, proudly displayed on its own coat of arms, must have sounded warmly familiar to someone from Liberia: "Liberty and Prosperity." The coat of arms even had a plow.

Tamba and his siblings were home.

They reunited with Henry and met his wife, their new stepmother, and then whisked up the Jersey Turnpike. Once again, they found themselves passing through miles of swamps, only this time they were doing it on an eight-lane interstate highway at a brisk sixty-five miles per hour—on their way to beginning their new life in a town called Teaneck.

If it seemed to Tamba that Teaneck was the center of the universe, he could be forgiven. The town was situated between major roads—Interstate 95, which runs from Maine to Florida, and Interstate 80, which begins in Teaneck and runs twenty-nine hundred miles across the country before rolling up in San Francisco. A few miles to the east, the George Washington Bridge waited to carry you across the Hudson River and into New York City. From Teaneck, he surely felt, you could go anywhere.

All the possibilities, all the choices . . . It all took a little getting used to for Tamba. How many food options could there be, he wondered? How many different pizza toppings do you really need? What does an eleven-year-old boy need with so many clothes? Back in Liberia, wardrobe options were a bit more limited and they never thought twice about it. "We walked around barefoot or wore sandals—if you had sandals," Tamba said. "You'd have shorts on but we went shirtless the majority of the time. We didn't have the means to have too many clothes, so we'd wear the same thing most of the time."

They were about as far from materialistic as kids could be. Still, their stepmother made sure they had new clothes and other staples they would need as they settled into their new surroundings.

Video games were new to Tamba (a fun first discovery—especially Doom). The prevalence of television was new, too. He even was shocked to see women driving cars; back in Liberia, that was a privilege reserved for men.

Every once in a while, Tamba would even find a little money had been left for him, a reward for helping clean his room or straighten up the house.

Occasionally, there would be twenty dollars for the children to buy themselves something—that was nearly as much money as it cost to buy their freedom at the checkpoint into Ivory Coast.

The transition wasn't always smooth. For a long time, Tamba and his siblings would flinch every time they heard a plane overhead—which, when you live under some of the busiest airspace on the planet, was pretty often. He would hear the roar of the engines and brace for gunfire that would never come.

A sudden loud noise, maybe just the slamming shut of a car door, would trigger a response they had learned living through a war. They would have to resist the impulse to drop to the ground, lie flat on their stomachs, even tuck their heels low so that absolutely no part of their body would show itself above the top of the grass.

"I always had that feeling," Tamba said. "I'm not sure we accepted the fact that we had escaped."

Everywhere he looked, things were different. This was, after all, New Jersey, and Tamba had never been exposed to a community made up of so many people from so many places.

The white faces he saw all around him certainly were new. The accents from Asia and the Caribbean were different and exotic and confusing. Even the African Americans that he saw were somehow unfamiliar. They tended to be African by heritage, American by birth. Even in the midst of diversity, Tamba felt like he stuck out.

Without question, the most challenging new experience was school. When the war began in Liberia, Tamba had just reached the age when children typically would start to go to school. But he was able to attend only infrequently the first year or two—most of his early education came from a life spent hiding in the bush, not in a classroom or from books.

Ah, books.

Tamba Hali had survived bullets and bombs, bugs in the bush, even the molasses-legged bureaucracy that left him in limbo as he waited to be accepted into the United States. Now that he was in America, in an American school, he was faced with a new enemy: books. Tamba did not know how to read or write.

We're not talking about struggling with some spelling, not knowing when to use an apostrophe, or the relationship between a silent E and long vowel sounds. He hadn't been introduced to any of it, not his ABC's or 123's.

"When I got into school and I was not able to read or write, it was shocking and humbling," Tamba said.

Tamba wasn't a very talkative kid to begin with. He was soft-spoken. Not like Saah, who was more outgoing, more comfortable interacting and connecting with new people. But here, as the new kid in Benjamin Franklin Middle School—the one with the heavy West African accent and an inability to read or write—Tamba became even more quiet and guarded.

When he listened to kids around his age, his mind would swim. They spoke so fast, had such command over what they wanted to say, Tamba's ears couldn't keep up. It wasn't a matter of not knowing the words; he struggled just to pick out the individual words as they whooshed by.

Enter Gail Dunn. Officially, she was the school's reading specialist. In reality, she was Tamba Hali's first coach.

At first, the school didn't know what to do with him. Tamba was eleven years old when he arrived at Benjamin Franklin. He was old enough for sixth grade, but he was so unprepared academically that they easily could have started him in elementary school. But that would not have been a beneficial fit for him socially.

He didn't need to be in a special-education

program because he was not a student with any special needs or learning disabilities. He simply had been deprived of schooling. The fact that he spoke English certainly helped, but it also meant that the track designed for traditional ESL (English as a Second Language) students was not the right fit, either.

So the school administrators placed him in a fifth-grade classroom—Benjamin Franklin is a middle school with students in fifth through eighth grades—and assigned him to Mrs. Dunn.

Every day, Tamba would leave his classroom (fifth and sixth grades at Benjamin Franklin were single-teacher classrooms, like in an elementary school; seventh and eighth were departmentalized, with kids changing classes for every subject) and spend an hour in Mrs. Dunn's reading room. It was a small room, without any desks—not unlike the typical Liberian schoolroom. They would sit together at a table and together they would begin Tamba's journey as a reader.

"We started with the basics: the alphabet, phonics, basic sight vocabulary," said Mrs. Dunn, who worked with Saah, too.

Even that wasn't easy, since most middle-school reading rooms don't have materials for new readers. Those resources belonged at the elementary schools. Fortunately, Mrs. Dunn had a friend who taught first grade in nearby Plainfield who sent along materials she could use with Tamba.

Because of his age, intelligence, and general aptitude for learning, Tamba picked up the basics quickly. What he learned from Mrs. Dunn was reinforced at home, where he spent hours and hours immersed in the Hooked on Phonics program provided by his father.

Remember—Henry Hali was a teacher. He taught chemistry at Teaneck High School and also at Fairleigh Dickinson University, which had a campus in Teaneck, right on the banks of the Hackensack River. He invested in the Hooked on Phonics materials, which included flash cards and illustrated workbooks and cassette tapes (ask your parents . . . they'll remember . . .) featuring lessons set to music that made them easier to remember.

The products were marketed well, with the easiest of phone numbers to learn (1-800-ABCDEFG) and the catchiest slogan, delivered in the commercials by an adorable, happy preschooler in pigtails: "Hooked on Phonics worked for me!"

"Those cards were hard," Saah recalled. "If you can't recognize the words, you feel like they're trying to torture you."

However, Hooked on Phonics worked for Tamba and Saah, and so did the dedicated efforts of Gail Dunn. As Tamba progressed, she made sure to find materials that were age appropriate. The adventures of Dick and Jane don't hold the interest of many eleven-year-old boys.

In the forty-six years she would work as an educator, thirty-six of which were spent in the Teaneck school district, Mrs. Dunn never had a challenge like the one she faced with Tamba and Saah. Once, she worked with a Japanese student who had moved from Japan, a supersmart kid who spoke no English. But that was a different situation. At least he had a foundation, albeit in another language.

With Tamba, Mrs. Dunn had to start from scratch. Soon enough, though, he was reading. He would read aloud the words on the signs his father pointed to when they were driving somewhere together. Eventually, he began to read books on his own. He still can remember the joy he found on the pages of the first Goosebumps book he finished.

"The story was so interesting," he said. "I read the whole thing, and then it was like, now what?"

A door had been opened for Tamba, who remains an avid reader and still loves to write—though he says that sometimes even now, in his thirties, he still feels like he's catching up. Together, he and Mrs. Dunn wrote a happy ending, even if developing Tamba's reading skills was not what Mrs. Dunn remembers most from their time together at her teaching table. It was his dedication and determination.

"I never saw him be afraid of anything," she said. "He was learning something completely new, and he decided he was going to be like all the other kids. At that age, that's really important—to be able to fit in and do what everybody else can do."

CHAPTER 6

A WHOLE NEW BALL GAME

Learning to read would remove one of the major obstacles that kept Tamba from fitting in with his new middle-school classmates. He brought down other barriers with a different weapon: a ball.

Tamba didn't play sports much during his childhood in Gbarnga. The opportunity didn't exist, nor did the infrastructure. Maybe the kids would find an old, worn soccer ball to kick around from time to time; if a nice new ball somehow found its way into the village, only the adults would be allowed to use it. Often, the children had to fashion a ball by taping paper together or using a grapefruit.

There certainly weren't organized leagues like the ones that exist in the United States.

"We didn't have a team to play on," Saah said. "If you wanted to join a team, you joined the rebel forces. That is your team. An AK-47 becomes your soccer ball."

Tamba didn't join any organized sports leagues when he first arrived in New Jersey. "More study, less play" was the tone set in Henry Hali's household, but Tamba and his siblings managed to find time to play. Usually with a real soccer ball.

Big Tamba was pretty good at soccer. So was Saah, who would go on to play soccer at Caldwell College (now Caldwell University), an NCAA Division II program about twenty miles from home. They would take Tamba to Votee Park, just across

Route 4 from Teaneck High School, to play in the neighborhood pickup soccer games.

From the start, Tamba showed athletic promise. And he flashed some soccer skills, too.

"I'll tell you this," Saah said. "He had very good foot skills. And he can dribble."

But it was dribbling another kind of ball that Tamba was drawn to. He had become enamored with basketball.

In 1995, the basketball world was aquiver over Michael Jordan's return to the NBA. The great Air Jordan had decided to come back to basketball, in the wake of a short-lived experiment in minor-league baseball. (Hey—even the greatest athletes need to find new ways to challenge themselves.) He left basketball abruptly in 1993 after leading the Chicago Bulls to three straight championships, and he would win another three in a row upon returning. The return of His Airness re-energized basketball fans across the country.

If there was one American athlete the children of Africa would have been aware of, even in the midst of a civil war, it was Michael Jordan. So many of the Liberian children who found themselves in the refugee camps of Sierra Leone and Guinea were clothed in donations sent from the States. Overwhelmingly, the most common jersey delivered through clothing drives at that time was the Chicago Bulls' number 23.

"When Tamba got hooked on basketball, all the kids were into Michael Jordan," Gail Dunn said.

Dreaming about becoming the next Michael Jordan might have been the first truly American thing Tamba had ever done. Finally, he had something in common with his classmates.

Fitting in had been a struggle for Tamba, more than it was for Saah. For some reason, one of the more popular kids at school befriended Saah from the start. "I shot straight to the top of the totem pole," he said. Tamba did not find such an ally.

In fact, the first interaction on his first day of school was a fight. A boy made an insulting comment about Tamba's mother—pretty standard fare for a middle-school hallway—and Tamba hit him. Ironically, that boy became one of Tamba's better friends, helping him through much of those first two years of school. But there were other insults and other fights. He was an easy target, who looked and sounded like no one else in the class.

Then he started to play soccer and basketball. He and Saah would play together in a lot of two-on-two games on the courts at the local playground, with Tamba showing a knack for a big-man's game. He was comfortable in a power-forward role—posting up around the basket, defending the rim, battling for rebounds . . . much more Karl Malone than Michael Jordan.

He began to recognize some of the kids from school at the playground. They would play together, and slowly Tamba started to win them over with energy and effort so different from his usual gentle nature.

Soon his classmates began picking him to be on their teams in gym class. It wasn't too much longer before he started being one of the first players picked.

"It was alarming to me that people wanted me to be on their team," Tamba said. "People started coming around."

Sports became Tamba's entry point into his new world. The insults didn't stop entirely. Neither did the fighting. Slowly but surely, though, Tamba was finding his way. He was developing a new set of skills, discovering things that he had no idea he was good at. He was gaining confidence in the classroom and finding friends through the games he was playing. His new life was taking root.

Roots provide stability, a foundation—even protection, as Tamba once learned the hard way. But they don't dictate the direction a life may grow in. As he prepared to head to high school, Tamba Hali's life was about to change again. In a direction he had never dreamed of.

CHAPTER 7

PUT YOUR HAND ON THE GROUND AND GO

Shortly after they had arrived in America, the Hali family found themselves in a car, driving through some nearby North Jersey community. Looking out the window that early autumn evening, the kids spotted something they had never seen before.

Banks of bright lights towered over metal bleachers that bordered a stunning green rectangle. Perfect straight lines spaced at precise intervals may have been painted across the length of this perfect lawn, some of which would have been straddled by numbers, making the whole thing look like a ruler a hundred yards long. Saah can't remember for sure; it may have been just a practice on an unfinished field or it may have been an actual game.

An actual football game.

What Saah does remember are the white jerseys. Set against the pure green backdrop, the white glowed, the light from above bouncing off them the way sunlight dances on gentle water. It was the first glimpse he and his half brother, Tamba, would have of American football.

Love at first sight this was not. In fact, it left little impression on Tamba whatsoever. His father, Henry, mentioned something along the lines of "That sport is very violent," and Tamba's attention turned elsewhere. After all, everything the kids saw these days was new to their eyes. A high-school football team really was no different from the Fuddruckers hamburger restaurant on Route 4 in Paramus. Everything was part of this brand-new American landscape, and the Hali children were soaking it all in.

If Tamba came to the United States knowing nothing about reading and writing, he knew even less about football. At least he knew that words existed. Football was nowhere on his radar before moving to Teaneck, and barely registered more than the occasional curious blip for the first few years after he arrived.

Surely, he was aware of it. You can't live eleven miles from Giants Stadium, an eighty-thousand-seat facility parked right next to the southbound lanes of the Jersey Turnpike, and not be aware of football. It was the only building in the country home to two National Football League franchises—the New York Giants and the New York Jets (yes, they are both New York teams though their shared stadium sits squarely in the swamps of Jersey). Not knowing would have been impossible.

Not caring . . . that's a different thing. Tamba's plate was already full, mostly with Hooked on Phonics flash cards and Michael Jordan dreams. Football was less than an afterthought. Once, when football appeared on a television screen he was watching, entirely by chance, Tamba commented on the size of the shoulders of the men who played the game. He hadn't realized that the players were wearing shoulder pads.

It never occurred to Tamba to give the game a try. Not until it was suggested to him by Ed Klimek, a physical-education teacher at Benjamin Franklin Middle School. Klimek had just been hired as an assistant coach at Teaneck High School, and he mentioned Tamba to the head coach, Dennis Heck.

"He said that kids were always picking on him and there were fights, but that Tamba was very raw and athletic and we should convince him to come out and play for us," Heck said.

"And that he knew nothing about football."

Klimek and Heck made their pitch to Tamba, who decided to give it a shot. He agreed. Just like that, Tamba would play for the Teaneck Highwaymen as a high-school freshman.

When he worked with Mrs. Dunn, Tamba took to the ABC's pretty quickly. The complicated Xs and Os of football were another story.

Basketball and soccer, the two sports he loved and was most familiar with, are played on the fly. Sure, there are plays and strategy, but those games have an organic flow to them. Most of the time, you react to a nonstop sequence of evolving game situations with minimal opportunity to plan ahead.

Football was entirely different. A play would be called in the huddle, the players would walk to the line, the ball would be snapped, the players would do the one or two things they were assigned to do on that play, then they'd go back to the huddle and do it all over again. This structure was foreign to Tamba and, usually, frustrating.

"I didn't realize that in football I would have to memorize plays," he said.

Every time he and his teammates broke the huddle, Tamba would have to ask the guy next to him, "What do I do?" At that time, he was an offensive right tackle, a blocker whose job was either to protect the quarterback or open holes in the defense for a running back. Typically, the right side is considered the strong side of an offense; the majority of a team's running plays are called to go to the right side. For much of his first season, Tamba had to rely on the right guard—the lineman lined up to his immediate left—to remind him what his job was and point out which of the guys lined up across from them he was responsible for blocking.

Once he knew what to do, he showed a natural ability to do it. As was the case in soccer, Tamba displayed good balance and footwork. And just as he did as a basketball power forward, Tamba demonstrated a taste for physical contact. He quickly came to like everything about the football experience: specifically, putting on the pads and running into someone.

Before the start of his sophomore season, Tamba grew. His oldest brother was still Big Tamba (and would always be), but Little Tamba was becoming a bigger Tamba. A stronger and faster Tamba, too. He would turn sixteen years old late that season, and he had already grown to about six foot one, 170 pounds.

Still, Tamba remembers being discouraged before that season began. He saw that there were bigger, better, more experienced offensive linemen, which likely would compromise his playing time. He never watched the game growing up; he certainly didn't want to start watching it from the Teaneck sidelines.

When Coach Heck moved him to the defensive side of the ball, Tamba became encouraged. At least he'd be out on the field. And when he started to learn the responsibilities of his new position on the defensive line, he became ecstatic.

"I embraced that part of the game," he said. "I got to run around and chase the guy with the ball. That was fun."

No longer did Tamba have to worry about the intricacies of pass protection or a run-blocking scheme. Coach Heck gave him one rule to remember in those early days of his position transition: "Don't let this game be confusing. Just put your hand on the ground and go."

That was it. "Put your hand on the ground and go." Instructions so short and sweet they could've fit inside a fortune cookie.

Coach Heck spent the next three years reminding Tamba of that simplest of mission statements. After Tamba went on to play college ball, if he ever found himself struggling, he would hear those words echoing in his memory and get himself back on track. Even when he reached the National Football League, the mantra remained top of mind. In 2015, Coach Heck visited him on the sidelines in Kansas City—the first game at Arrowhead Stadium that Coach had ever attended. The Chiefs had gotten off to a slow start that season, losing five of their first six games. Before that late-October home game against the Pittsburgh Steelers, Tamba came over to greet his old coach with a handshake and a smile. Coach pulled him close for a second and delivered his eight-word pep talk to his prized pupil: "Put your hand on the ground and go."

(For the record, Tamba Hali got 2 sacks that game, including one that caused a fumble and ended Pittsburgh's last desperate bid for a comeback. The Chiefs would win that game and the next nine in a row to qualify for the playoffs, then extended their streak to eleven games with an opening-round win at Houston).

As a high-school sophomore, Tamba lived by those words. He felt right at home with his hand on the ground. And, boy, could he go.

More than that, he just wouldn't stop.

Early in his sophomore season, Teaneck traveled up to play St. Joseph Regional, a traditional powerhouse located, fittingly, at the top of New Jersey, right along the New York border. The Green Knights were a monster, which made for some long nights for anyone unlucky enough to wind up on their schedule. At various points during that 1999 season, SJR was ranked number one in the state of New Jersey and as high as number seven in the *USA Today* national rankings.

The Highwaymen got hammered, 36–0. But you would never have known it from watching Tamba Hali. The teams may have been mismatched, but for the first time Tamba was showing that he belonged on the same field as the big boys.

"These parochial schools come with a reputation, and here I am, a sophomore, and I'm hitting them. They're staring me down, as if I'm supposed to stop. I didn't understand it," Tamba said. "I found a lot of joy being out there on the field."

Tamba played like that the rest of his sophomore season. And people noticed. After his first season playing defense—only his second season of playing football period—he was named first-team All-Northern New Jersey Interscholastic League Division A, a mouthful of an honor but a nice surprise.

A far bigger one came from a little farther north. The football coaches from Boston College wrote a letter to Tamba, offering him a full scholarship. That wasn't just stunning. "It's unheard of," Coach Heck said.

Unfathomable. It had never occurred to Tamba

that playing sports could create such opportunities. Sure, he would have liked to be the next Michael Jordan, but he'd never really thought about how to go about doing that. College might have been part of some far-off plan (surely for Henry it was), but it certainly was not something he was thinking about as a sophomore. And the prospect of playing college football certainly hadn't even occurred to him.

"I wasn't aware that you could get scholarships or make money playing this game," Tamba said.

He declined Boston College's lightning bolt of an offer. But it was official: Tamba Hali was on the recruiting radar, which meant more attention would be coming. More offers, too. It was time to plan and prepare for the next step. The first sacrifice was going to be a tough one.

"Between his sophomore and junior year, I told him he couldn't play basketball the next season," Coach Heck said.

So much for becoming the heir to Air Jordan. Reluctantly, Tamba agreed. He knew that Coach Heck had worked with a couple of players who had gone on to the NFL, including Dave Szott, whom Heck coached at Clifton High School before taking over at Teaneck. Szott played offensive guard for fourteen professional seasons and was wrapping up a decade-long run in Kansas City while Tamba was weighing the BC offer. Tamba trusted Heck and put basketball on the shelf for a year. Instead, he would focus on football and the weight training he would need to do in order to ramp up his development.

When Tamba showed up for his junior season, Heck knew something special was on the horizon. He saw it right away. He was impressed by Tamba's physical condition and marveled at his work ethic. Every sprint he ran at practice he wanted to finish first. Every drill the team did he wanted to be first in line. Football scouts and analysts talk admiringly about a player's "motor." Tamba's never stopped purring.

In team meetings, the Highwaymen would watch films of their previous games. Coach Heck would stop the film whenever teaching points presented themselves. Much of the time, these moments were examples set by Tamba. Heck loved to point out Tamba's toughness. "This kid never played football before in his life," he would say, rewinding and reviewing any number of plays, "and he still has the audacity to run over this kid."

At practice, Heck had to force Tamba to sit out plays from time to time. Tamba neither needed nor asked for a break. But he had to take a knee so Teaneck's offense could get some work done. Whenever he lined up against them, they couldn't block him. Neither could anybody else.

He was developing a reputation as the fearless fighter Mrs. Dunn had seen in the reading room.

He was afraid of nothing on the football field—and after what he'd witnessed in the killing fields of Liberia, how could he be? To some players, football was life or death; Tamba Hali had seen enough death to know better.

Instead, he played the game without fear. He played with humility. He wasn't concerned with the reporters or the rankings or the college recruiting rumors. The attention he was starting to get meant nothing to him.

"I was getting attention for football, but it didn't go to my head. I didn't understand what was so good about playing sports," he said. "I was just excited to play in the games and to be around the guys."

Despite all the individual accolades piling up around him, Tamba remained the quintessential team player—any coach's dream. He happily lined up wherever Coach Heck put him, whether it was defensive end, defensive tackle, nose guard, or even linebacker. The Teaneck coaches loved to move him around and make the other team have to find number 72 at the start of every play.

Heck once attended a clinic featuring Rex Ryan (future head coach of the New York Jets and Buffalo Bills) and his father, Buddy Ryan, the legendary defensive coordinator for the 1985 Chicago Bears, often considered the best defense in NFL history. At that clinic, the Ryans taught the concepts of the 46 Defense (Buddy's signature system). Heck came away with the understanding that a coach might want to line up his most disruptive player head-on against the center. You needed to put someone there who would be impossible to block, they said, someone who could penetrate the heart of an offensive line and blow up the quarterback's plan right along with his pocket of protection.

Heck had a guy who could do just that.

"We would line up Tamba over center and he

would just give that guy fits. They just couldn't handle him," Coach Heck said. "It had nothing to do with his body. It was all about his heart. Some people have that drive, that heart, that motor, and they're never going to quit. When you have to play against that every play, it's exhausting."

Tamba's junior season played out like one continuous highlight reel. When it was over, he was first-team all-state, being recruited by major college football programs from across the country. Three years earlier, Tamba Hali thought getting a quarter back meant receiving change from a cashier. Now, he was a quarterback hunter, one of the most sought-after defensive prospects in America.

Even Henry Hali was becoming a football fan.

Tamba's senior season was more of the same: dominant performances on the field, mounting interest off it. Coach Heck remembers one sequence of three plays that pretty much summed up the kind of player Tamba had become.

It was Thanksgiving, which around Teaneck meant more than turkey and stuffing. The holiday was home to the annual rivalry game between Teaneck and Hackensack, a tradition dating back to 1931. It was always the regular-season finale, and Teaneck had lost the previous three meetings.

The Highwaymen led by a touchdown, 14–7, late in the game. The Comets were moving the ball, and tension in the stands was rising like the mercury in the meat thermometers jabbed into turkeys all over Bergen County. Tamba stopped three plays in a row, making tackles on two running plays and getting a sack on Hackensack's last play.

Tamba Hali stamped his signature on the last three plays of his high-school career. The kid who had to be introduced to football when he first arrived at Teaneck now walked off the field as perhaps the best player in Highwaymen history. He certainly was one of the most decorated.

He was honored as an all-state and All-America

selection and nominated as the Gatorade Player of the Year in the state of New Jersey. *SuperPrep*, a well-established recruiting service, considered him the best prospect in New Jersey—at any position—and the third-best defensive-line prospect in the country.

Forget Michael Jordan. Tamba Hali was making a name for himself.

CHAPTER 8

"I WANT TO WEAR THAT UNIFORM"

"I am a Texas player, and Texas is my home state."

That's how Vince Young, as reported by *Sports Illustrated*, once described his decision to sign with the University of Texas. Young, a quarterback who could run as well as he could throw, made his mark at Madison High School in Houston. He was the national high-school Player of the Year in the eyes of the people who rank such things and universally considered the prize catch in the 2002 recruiting class.

He was the best that Texas high-school football

had to offer that year, and Texas was the natural choice. The *only* choice. When you grow up immersed in the Texas football culture and the Longhorns come calling, your decision about where to go to college and play your college football is essentially a no-brainer. Some even call it a dream come true.

Tamba Hali had no such dreams growing up.

"When I was five or six, maybe the dream was to become a soldier," Tamba said. "We were worried about getting our next meal; we really couldn't dream at that time. Reality was too real for us to think beyond what was happening. I really couldn't imagine anything."

So when Boston College offered Tamba a scholarship after his sophomore season at Teaneck High School, he really didn't know what to think or how to react. He had to ask his coach, Dennis Heck, "What do I say to the man?" This was not something he had always dreamed might happen to him. He wasn't even aware that it possibly could.

He started to appreciate his new reality when offers started pouring in during his breakout junior season. Two dozen or so schools had expressed interest in having Tamba come learn on their campus and play football for their team.

By the end of his senior season, Hali was one of the most enthusiastically pursued prospects in the country. Maybe not quite at Young's level (quarterbacks have always existed on a different plane), but enough to make him a familiar name on the wish lists of college fans from gray upstate New York to golden Southern California. According to the National Federation of State High School Associations, 853,537 kids had played 11-v-11 high-school football in 2001. Tamba Hali was considered among the top fifty to sixty seniors in the land.

Sixty-four scholarship offers were extended to Tamba. And everyone waited to see which one he would accept.

The NCAA allows high-school seniors to make "official" visits to as many as five different campuses. Official visits mean the recruit is brought in as an official guest of the university, and his meal and travel expenses are paid for. Recruits are allowed to take as many unofficial visits—when they pay their own way—as they'd like. Tamba's five visits were to USC, Syracuse, Miami, Maryland, and Penn State.

But it was a visit from college football royalty that swayed Tamba's decision. In late January 2002, Joe Paterno, head coach at Penn State University, came to Teaneck to see Tamba and pitch him in person.

He had already handwritten a six-page letter to Tamba—which Coach Heck, now the principal at Teaneck High School, still keeps in a drawer in his desk. Tamba read as much of the letter as he could before the cursive letters became too tiring to decipher. Now, Coach Paterno was sitting in

Coach Heck's office, waiting to talk to Tamba.

Tamba wanted to look good for the meeting, so he had one of his friends braid his long hair. The start of a new class period or something must have interrupted them because Tamba showed up for the meeting sporting only half a head of braided hair. Like everything else in Tamba's life—football and academics—there was still work to be done.

Coach Paterno was a seventy-five-year-old man at the time, with thirty-five seasons as Penn State's head coach already under his belt. He didn't know what to make of Tamba's hairdo. But he was anxious to make an impression of his own.

"Joe says to Tamba, 'You know, I could pick up that phone, call anybody in the country, and they'll return my call,'" Coach Heck said. "Tamba said, 'Okay.' Joe says, 'I mean, I can call any coach in the NFL and they'll return my call.' Tamba said, 'That's great.' 'I could call the president of the United States and he'd return my call.' He was trying to get across to Tamba that he had a great deal of influence."

Tamba's reaction was similar to Paterno's reaction to his hair. He wasn't sure how to respond.

"So Tamba says, 'I really like your uniforms.'" Heck said. "'I want to wear that uniform.'"

The decision really didn't come down to the uniforms, although it would have made perfect sense. There really isn't a more modest, less individual-focused fashion statement in all of sports than the one made by the Nittany Lions. For home games, they wear navy blue jerseys so dark that it looks like the players' bodies are hiding in the shadows and white pants that could have been designed to show a maximum amount of grass stains, dirt, blood, and streaks of opponents' helmet paint (so you can tell by a guy's pants how hard he worked that day). For road games, it's white tops and white bottoms, as if to suggest nothing special has come to town. They were almost invisible.

The helmet, of course, is plain white, ordinary

white, with a single blue streak bisecting what otherwise might look like an egg to be cracked. The helmet has no logo on it, just as the jersey has no name on it—no player's name on the back, no school name on the front, no branding on the sleeves. Every time a player dresses for a game, he is reminded by one peek in the mirror that he is no different from everyone around him in the locker room, that he is no greater or lesser a piece to the Penn State puzzle than any of his teammates, no more special or unique than the players who wore this same jersey and helmet and pants before or those who will wear it after their time is done.

And don't forget the black shoes. Legend has it that Joe Paterno went for the black shoes because they make his players look slower. It's subtle and strategic and might perhaps result in the slightest of advantages at some point during some game someday. What it's not is flashy, which is why the Penn State look probably appealed to Tamba.

But it's not why he made his decision. Ultimately, he chose Penn State over his second choice, Syracuse, after much discussion and deliberation with Henry and with Coach Heck.

"Tamba came to me when it was time to make his decision," Heck said. "He says, 'Coach, I don't know where to go. Where would you send your son?'"

Tamba had become like a son to Heck, whose own children had become close with his best player. He appreciated the physicality and relentlessness Tamba brought to the football field almost as much as the gentle respect with which he treated people off it.

Together, son and coach and father arrived at the decision. On January 29, 2002, Tamba announced his verbal commitment. On February 6, he signed his letter of intent and submitted it by fax machine (again . . . ask your parents . . .). Eight years after learning to read and write, Tamba Hali was going to college. Four years after he first tucked his own shoulders into a pair of shoulder pads, he was going to play college football. At Pennsylvania State University.

Ten years after he stepped silently past that dead body at the border, leaving behind a country being ripped apart, Tamba was going to a place known as Happy Valley.

CHAPTER 9

THE END GAME

For a few final, violent months of 2003, war raged on in Liberia. This was not the Liberian civil war that Tamba Hali and his siblings had lived through and eventually fled. That war ended in 1997, when Charles Taylor, the leader of the rebellious National Patriotic Front of Liberia, was voted president in a general election overseen by observers from the United Nations. The rally cry for the hundreds of thousands of Liberians who supported the man who plunged their country into war before plundering its resources was unlike any candidate's campaign slogan before or since: "He killed my ma, he killed my pa, I'll vote for him!"

By 1999, war had erupted again. It was called the Second Liberian Civil War, but it was really a continuation of the one Taylor and his rebel forces had started on Christmas Day a decade earlier.

Rachel Keita, Tamba Hali's mother, was still in danger. She had returned to Monrovia, where she worked as a minister, trying to help heal the people and the city, even as the fighting continued around her. In 2003, as she walked with three friends through the streets of Liberia's murdered capital, bullets rang out without warning. Nonspecific news reports acknowledged that at least one of Rachel's friends had been killed. Rachel had been shot in the knee but survived.

For most of the first ten years of his life, Tamba lived without his father. For all of the second ten years, he lived without his mother. He had always hoped to find a way to bring her to America, just as his father had managed to do for him and his brothers and sister. Now that he was playing college football and developing into a potential professional prospect, a plan was starting to materialize.

If he could make it to the NFL, Tamba figured, he could afford to rescue his mother from Liberia. And he *had* to get her out.

Tamba had never had a plan for football before, no idea what he wanted to get out of it. He had to be talked into playing the game in the first place, but he'd never considered that it might carry him to college or beyond. Now, here he was at Penn State, playing for the legendary and influential Joe Paterno; perhaps it was time to consider what other miracles football could conjure up.

Back in high school, Tamba never gave much thought to what outsiders were saying about his performance or his potential. As he said, "I didn't do it for anyone else but me." It started to occur to him that he really did have something else to play for, some*one* else to play for.

His mother.

College wasn't always easy for Tamba. Not in the classroom, for starters. The support staff he had back in Teaneck, his father, Henry, in particular, was gone, and he was forced to make schoolwork a priority and tackle it on his own—a lesson familiar to pretty much all college freshmen. He dropped a class that would be taught largely online because that kind of structure didn't feel comfortable to him. He switched majors a time or two (or three) and found tutors when he needed them. He still felt like he was behind in his schooling, but falling behind was not an option. Not in Joe Paterno's world. Tamba persevered and soon he was making academic progress.

The challenges of college extended to the field, too. Tamba learned pretty quickly that the Big Ten Conference wasn't quite as easy to dominate as the high-school competition back in Jersey.

"I started to realize there's another level of playing that you have to get to," he said. "Your natural ability is not going to let you take over games like you did in high school. You had to be able to do it where guys around you are as good as you or better."

Tamba spent his first two college seasons playing defensive tackle, which meant he was going up against a steady rotation of three-hundred-pound guards who would wind up in the NFL: Iowa's Eric Steinbach (second round draft pick, 2003), Illinois's David Diehl (fifth round, 2003), Ohio State's Alex Stepanovich (fourth round, 2004), and Michigan's David Baas (second round, 2005).

Then, in 2004, Hali moved to defensive end. And everything changed. He earned second-team All–Big Ten honors and was maturing into a first-rate defender. Just as attention swarmed him back in high school like ants on a fallen sandwich at a picnic, the NFL Draft world began to speculate about his future.

"I only had two sacks that year, but I played well enough according to my coaches that I could have been drafted in the third or fourth round," Tamba said.

In truth, he never dreamed of leaving college after that junior season. He easily could have, considering the difficult state of Penn State football. The Nittany Lions went 3–9 during his sophomore season, 4–7 during his junior season—the worst back-to-back stretch of seasons in school history—and even the true blue-and-white faithful were beginning to wonder whether Paterno had reached the end of his road.

Tamba's coaches told him that if he wanted to be recognized as one of the better players in the country, he would have to get sacks. They explained that people who can get to the quarterback—pass rushers—are held in unique esteem at the NFL level. They were nearly as valued as the quarterbacks they were sent to conquer.

There was more work to be done before Tamba could move on. So he stayed, committed to learning the little things that Coach Paterno always preached about to him.

"Joe always said, 'If you take care of the little things, the big things will take care of themselves.' It's the behind-the-scenes stuff that you do that makes them happen," Tamba said. "The little things that people overlook may not seem like a big deal. But if you can create good habits instead of bad habits, they will create who you are. They will set you up for success."

His senior season was an absolute success, for Tamba as well as his team. His impressive statistics (65 tackles, 11 sacks, 17 tackles for loss) brought impressive awards (Big Ten Defensive Player of the Year, first-team All-America). Penn State returned to prominence in a big way, going 11–1, winning the Big Ten Conference and the Orange Bowl, and finishing number three in the final national rankings.

Perhaps the most important play of the season had Tamba's fingerprints all over it. The Lions had won their first five games of the season—already surpassing their win total from the year before. Ohio State came to State College, PA, ranked sixth in the country. Penn State led by a touchdown, 17–10, late in the fourth quarter, but the Buckeyes were driving. Just as he had done against Hackensack (and would do countless times in Kansas City), Tamba brought a heavy rush from the left side of the defensive line, picked up speed as he approached Troy Smith, and finally walloped the Buckeyes quarterback. He enveloped Smith— who would win the Heisman Trophy the following season—the way a bun envelops a hot dog. In doing so, he jarred loose the ball, which was recovered by another Penn State defender. The sack-and-forced-fumble combination was becoming the Tamba Hali Special.

That play essentially finished off Penn State's statement win. And when PSU and OSU were tied atop the Big Ten standings at the end of the regular season, that win broke the tie and gave the Nittany Lions the conference title, plus the corresponding berth to the Orange Bowl.

And yet when the play was done, while his teammates danced in celebration and 109,000 fans shook Beaver Stadium to its foundation, Tamba Hali took it in stride. Joyous pandemonium erupted around him, and he simply strode off the field, like a businessman walking out of a meeting. No high fives, no fist bumps, no posing for posterity in the middle of a moment that will live on in Penn State lore. He had done his job—he put his hand on the ground and he went and got the quarterback—but there was still work to do.

Over the next six months, Tamba worked

his plan. He went to the Senior Bowl in Mobile, Alabama—a postseason all-star showcase, where senior prospects would practice and play a game in front of every talent evaluator in the NFL. Tamba was the game's Defensive Most Valuable Player.

Soon after, he went to the NFL Scouting Combine in Indianapolis, where more than three hundred prospects are tested and measured and interviewed by NFL coaches and general managers and scouts. They timed him in the forty-yard dash, counted the number of times he could bench press 225 pounds, checked his height, weight, hand size, and wingspan. They subjected him to the Wonderlic intelligence test and a battery of probing interview questions. Tamba performed well enough there to move himself into consideration for a first-round pick.

Sure enough, in April, the Kansas City Chiefs invested their first-round pick—the twentieth overall pick in the 2006 NFL Draft—on Tamba Hali. His mission was nearly complete.

While Tamba worked the football end of things, he had a small army of influential friends working the diplomatic side. He was going to get Rachel out of West Africa. The fighting there had stopped back in the summer of 2003, so she wasn't in immediate danger, but Tamba and his mother had waited long enough.

Coach Paterno made the kind of calls he'd told Tamba about in Dennis Heck's office back in Teaneck, reaching out to any connections he had who could help speed along the process. His son, Scott, was an attorney and also worked vigorously on Tamba's behalf. Lamar Hunt, the owner of the Chiefs, pitched in, as did Carl Peterson, the Kansas City general manager who had spent his team's coveted first-round pick on Tamba on that second-to-last day in April.

Rick Santorum, a senator from Pennsylvania, pulled whatever strings he could in Washington, DC. So did Jack Kemp, a former congressman from New

York who was Bob Dole's running mate when Dole ran for president in 1996. Kemp also had been a professional quarterback, playing in the Canadian Football League, the American Football League, and even a few seasons in the National Football League in the late 1950s. His support was the rare example of a quarterback helping out a premier pass rusher.

Every button was pushed, every box checked . . . except one. And on July 31, 2006, the Chiefs gave their rookie defensive end a pass on practice, allowing Tamba to leave in the middle of two-a-days (now illegal summer training camp sessions that featured two padded practices a day) so he could fly from River Falls, Wisconsin, to Teaneck and be sworn in as a citizen of the United States.

With his status as a newly minted American and proof of a steady job (his first contract with the Chiefs would pay him more than ten million dollars over his first five years in the league), not to mention the diploma he'd received as a graduate from Penn State University, everything was in place. Tamba Hali now could afford and was legally able to bring his mother into the country. She was, after all, immediate family.

Rachel Keita arrived three weeks into her son's first season in the NFL. The first time she ever saw him play football, he picked up his first NFL sack.

"I do sit down and reflect at times, and I think things could have gone a whole different way," Tamba said. "What are the chances? The majority of kids I was around are dead. If my dad wasn't in the US, I was in Africa. Period. By the grace of God, I am still here. It is a blessing to me to be in the position I am in. Not just to have come to the US, but to play this sport."

HOME AGAIN

In the spring of 2016, Tamba Hali went home.

It had been almost twenty-two years since Tamba, Big Tamba, Saah, and Kumba boarded a flight that would carry them away to a new land and a new life. Much had changed over the decades, for both Liberia and Tamba.

Liberia, for thirteen years, had been living in peace. Charles Taylor was in prison, serving a fifty-year sentence for his role in war crimes committed against Liberia and Sierra Leone. Ellen Johnson

Sirleaf was ten years into her historic presidency; the people of Liberia made her the first woman to win a democratic election and serve as the head of state for an African country. She took office on January 16, 2006—less than two weeks after Tamba Hali played his final college football game, a 26–23 three-overtime win over Florida State in the Orange Bowl.

The population had surged to more than four million people, making it the fastest-growing country in the world. Poverty remained a widespread problem, and public health crises, such as the 2014 Ebola epidemic, posed significant challenges to a country piecing its infrastructure and government services back together. Still, Liberia was coming back to life.

There was much Tamba would not recognize in Liberia after all these years, starting with the paved roads that led him back to Gbarnga. And Liberia wouldn't recognize Tamba at all. He had changed in ways unimaginable and immeasurable since the last time he was inside his home country.

For starters, he was now a six-foot, three-inch, 275-pound, thirty-two-year-old man. He had put in ten years as a professional football player, and had been paid richly for them. (Tamba earned roughly sixty-five million dollars in salary between 2006 and 2015.) A month or so before his trip to Africa, he signed a new three-year contract worth twenty-one million dollars that could enable him to finish his career with the Kansas City Chiefs, the only NFL home he had ever known.

The time was right for a reunion.

Tamba's oldest brother, Big Tamba, had been back already. He visited in 2012 and decided that the next time he returned, he would have his brother with him.

Tamba's other older brother, Saah, had been back, too. Many times, in fact. His visits are not trips down memory lane but rather work-related missions. He goes back to work with the children, to help with schools that have opened in recent years. He wants their childhoods to be better than his was. He brings them brand-new soccer balls.

But this was Tamba's first trip, and he had to be shocked to find that his family's house in Gbarnga was still standing. So many homes had been destroyed during the war. Others were looted, stripped of every possession left behind. Anything that could be salvaged had been taken. Years later, families would return to find a skeleton that had been picked clean by vultures.

Tamba's house, though, was standing. You can hear the amazement in his voice when you watch the videos he shot on his phone and posted to his Instagram account. He tours the one-story cinder-block structure with the corrugated tin roof and memories flood through him.

He remembers the river they used to fish in. He remembers chasing and catching groundhogs by the banana bush. He remembers where he used to bathe, where the side entrance used to be, where his mother used to plant her garden.

And he remembers where he stood the first day the planes darkened the skies, their bullets peppering the ground, fatally wounding the innocence of all the children in the village.

On this visit, Tamba is surrounded by extended family, cousins mostly, who have returned to live in and around Gbarnga. They have heard stories about their long-lost cousin who had become a football player, but they might not have believed them until they saw him for themselves. The Chiefs T-shirt he wore, white with red lettering, completed the picture. He stood before them a strong, smiling symbol of the American Dream.

Over the few days he was in Liberia, Tamba made a few more stops. He visited the beach in Monrovia. He dropped by Hott FM 107.9, the most popular radio station among Liberia's young listeners. He even had a personal audience with President Ellen Johnson Sirleaf. It was the trip of a lifetime, a first chance to reconnect with the place he came from.

Soon, though, Tamba would return to America, where his immediate family has been living for years. He would get back to Kansas City and start preparing with his teammates for the upcoming season. He would return to his jujitsu training with the Gracie Academy gurus, putting in the necessary hard work to recover from off-season knee surgery and be ready to win the battles that define every play in every NFL game.

And on Sunday, September 11, he would strap on his cherry-red helmet and run out onto the field at Arrowhead Stadium, the home of the Chiefs, to begin his eleventh season. Here, in front of the cheering fans, sweating and stretching and striving with his teammates, Tamba Hali was back where he belonged.

Liberia was where he came from. It shaped the life he would lead. But here, lining up as the right outside linebacker for the Kansas City Chiefs, with his hand on the ground, ready to go after another quarterback, Tamba Hali was home.

ACKNOWLEDGMENTS

Gathering stories and experiences from Tamba Hali's unique and fascinating childhood and football career would not have been possible without his willing participation in this project. I am grateful to Tamba for his generosity with his time, his candor, and his cooperation. I also want to thank Tamba's family, who shared their time and memories with me—specifically, his brothers, Big Tamba and Saah. Much appreciation is due to two of the major influences in Tamba's life who were willing to talk and share stories: his devoted reading instructor, Gail Dunn, and his varsity football coach at Teaneck High School, Dennis Heck. And, of course,

I thank Jim Ivler of Sportstars, Tamba's agent who facilitated the conversation in the first place, and Pat Kirwan, who introduced the idea to Jim.

Also, I would like to thank my brothers-in-law, Matt Hochbrueckner and Eduardo Garcia-Rolland. Back in 2003—a dozen years before this project was born—they were living in Freetown, Sierra Leone, and provided an eye-opening tour of the rebuilding of that country after its own recent civil war. One day, we visited a refugee camp in Kenema, where thousands of Liberians had fled to escape the fighting across the border. That unforgettable visit helped inspire the desire to tell Tamba's story.

Finally, many thanks go out to Rick Richter at Aevitas Creative Management and to Fiona Simpson and Mara Anastas and their talented team at Simon & Schuster for their belief in and support for the Real Sports series from the start.

ABOUT THE AUTHOR

David Seigerman's love of sports was kindled on the ball fields of his Long Island childhood, then fanned while rooting for the Mets, Jets, and Rangers through some historically bad seasons in the 1970s and 1980s. Upon realizing that his best path to the big leagues would be not with a bat but with a pen, he graduated from Ithaca College a million years ago and began a career as a sports journalist. He has been thrilled by the privilege of covering games and telling stories about athletes across all levels of all sports—including the Super Bowl, World Series, Stanley Cup finals, Final Four, Women's World Cup, Triple Crown races—for pretty much every storytelling medium there is: newspapers, magazines, television, radio, digital, documentaries, and books. Prior to the Real Sports series, David coauthored several books, including *Take Your Eye Off the Ball: How to Watch Football by Knowing Where to Look*, and *Go Deeper: Quarterback: The Toughest Job in Pro Sports* (both with Pat Kirwan), and *Under Pressure: How Playing Football Almost Cost Me Everything and Why I'd Do It All Again* (with Ray Lucas). Aside from a goal scored in a beginner's men's ice-hockey league (February 7, 2013) and an honest-to-goodness hole in one (June 5, 2015—with witnesses), his most treasured sports moments have come from coaching and watching his daughter and son on the ball fields and skating rinks of their own Westchester County childhoods.

ABOUT REAL CONTENT MEDIA GROUP

Real Content Media Group creates, produces, and distributes content across all forms of media, including television, radio, Internet, OTT digital networks, social media, syndication, and publishing. We specialize in the seamless integration of content and products to form salable media brands that speak very clearly to targeted audiences. Using our strategic network, we currently distribute content, products, and services in the Sports and Health & Wellness verticals.